RECREATE DISCOVERIES ABOUT

FORCES

CRABTREE
PUBLISHING COMPANY
WWW.CRABTREEBOOKS.COM

ANNA CLAYBOURNE

RECREATE SCiENTiFiC DISCOVERIES

Author:
Anna Claybourne
Editorial director:
Kathy Middleton
Editors:
Sarah Silver
Elizabeth DiEmanuele
Proofreader:
Wendy Scavuzzo
Interior design:
Eoin Norton & Katherine Berti
Cover design:
Katherine Berti
Photo research:
Diana Morris
Print and production coordinator:
Katherine Berti

Images:
All images by Eoin Norton for Wayland except the following:
Alamy: Jam World Images: p. 23br
Getty Images
    Corbis via Getty Images: p. 26t
    Jeffrey Coolidge: p. 26b, 29b
    Leemage/UIGs: p. 6tl
    The Evening Standard/Hulton Archive: p. 18cl
Lin Emery/DACS, London/VAGA, NY 2017: p. 25bl
Renitenza Certissima dell' Aqua alla Compressione, R Magggiotti, 1648: 12c
Shutterstock: front cover (pinwheel, balloon, stationery), p. 11 br
    Aleksandr Kurganov: p. 19br
    Herbert/AP/Rex: p. 24t
    Ina van Hateren: p. 5t
    Jan Hindstroem : p. 4b
    Juan David Ferrando: front cover (car)
    Pat Falconer/REX: p. 7bc
    Paul Velgos: p. 17cr
    Pupes : p. 4t
    Sashkin: p. front cover (balls), 9b
    Steve Collender: p. 17tr
Theo Jansen/DACS, London 2017: 5b
Topfoto: Franz Hubmann/Imagno: p. 22tr
Wikimedia Commons: p. 10tr, 18tr
    BPK Berlin: p. 10cl
    Chemical Heritage Foundation. Photo by Will Brown/CC: p. 14tr
    Haags Historisch Museum: p. 8tr
    NMM Greenwich: p. 6tr
    TU- Braunschweig: p. 20tr
Every attempt has been made to clear copyright. Should there be any inadvertent omission please apply to the publisher for rectification.

Library and Archives Canada Cataloguing in Publication

Claybourne, Anna, author
    Recreate discoveries about forces / Anna Claybourne.

(Recreate scientific discoveries)
Includes index.
Issued in print and electronic formats.
ISBN 978-0-7787-5051-2 (hardcover).--
ISBN 978-0-7787-5064-2 (softcover).--
ISBN 978-1-4271-2150-9 (HTML)

    1. Force and energy--Experiments--Juvenile literature. I. Title.

QC73.4.C533 2018   j531'.6   C2018-902447-X
                                                        C2018-902448-8

Library of Congress Cataloging-in-Publication Data

Names: Claybourne, Anna, author.
Title: Recreate discoveries about forces / Anna Claybourne.
Description: New York, New York : Crabtree Publishing, 2019. |
    Series: Recreate scientific discoveries | Includes index.
Identifiers: LCCN 2018021343 (print) | LCCN 2018025447 (ebook) |
    ISBN 9781427121509 (Electronic) |
    ISBN 9780778750512 (hardcover) |
    ISBN 9780778750642 (pbk.)
Subjects: LCSH: Force and energy--Experiments--Juvenile literature. |
    Motion--Experiments--Juvenile literature.
Classification: LCC QC73.4 (ebook) | LCC QC73.4 .C51654 2019 (print) |
    DDC 531/.113--dc23
LC record available at https://lccn.loc.gov/2018021343

Crabtree Publishing Company

www.crabtreebooks.com   1-800-387-7650

Published in 2019 by Crabtree Publishing Company

First published in Great Britain in 2018 by Wayland
Copyright © Hodder and Stoughton, 2018

Published in Canada
Crabtree Publishing
616 Welland Ave.
St. Catharines, Ontario
L2M 5V6

Published in the United States
Crabtree Publishing
PMB 59051
350 Fifth Avenue, 59th Floor
New York, New York 10118

Note:
In preparation of this book, all due care has been exercised with regard to the instructions, activities and techniques depicted. The publishers regret that they can accept no liability for any loss or injury sustained. Always follow the manufacturers' advice when using electric and battery-powered appliances.

The website addresses (URLs) included in this book were valid at the time of going to press. It is possible that some addresses may have changed or sites may have changed or closed down since publication. While the author and publishers regret any inconvenience this may cause to the readers, no responsibility for any such changes can be accepted by either the author or the publishers.

Printed in the U.S.A./082018/CG20180601

CONTENTS

TAKE CARE!

These projects can be made with everyday objects, materials, and tools that you can find at home, or in a supermarket, hobby store, or DIY store. Some projects may involve working with things that are sharp or breakable, or need extra strength to operate. Make sure you have an adult on hand to supervise and to help with anything that could be dangerous. Always get permission before you try out any of the projects

UNDERSTANDING FORCES

Forces are around us all the time. Science lessons often describe forces as "pushes and pulls." They make all kinds of movements or actions happen.

It sounds simple because it is! For example, when you push the first domino in a row, the dominoes all topple down. This is because the force of one falling pushes the next one.

TYPES OF FORCES

Although all forces push or pull, they can do this in lots of ways, and there are many different types of forces. They include:

 Applied force— a direct push or pull on an object

Friction—a force that slows or stops objects when they rub together

Upthrust—a force that makes something float because the liquid it is in pushes up

 Gravity—a force that pulls objects to each other, even if they're not touching

 Electric force— A force created when objects are electrically charged

 Air resistance—a slowing force that happens when an object moves through air

Throwing an object involves many forces working at once.

MANY FORCES

Forces work in all kinds of ways, not just one at a time. In this picture, you can see several forces in action.

1. **Pushing force of your arm**

2. **Pulling force of gravity**

3. **Slowing force of air resistance**

4. **Friction force when the object hits the ground**

FORCE INVENTIONS

Forces play an important part in human inventions. We use forces to help us do jobs in an easier way.

Think of the greatest invention of all time: the wheel. The wheel makes it much easier to move things around. We also use machines, tools, and gadgets to do everyday jobs. Without force, nothing would move at all.

A water wheel uses the force of falling water to create a turning force.

FORCES IN ART

Artists often use force to create their art. In the past, art needed to stay still until it was complete. It took a good understanding of forces to make sculptures and other things.

Art itself did not display forces in action until more recently. Now, more and more art needs forces to work. Some artists make art that requires natural forces, such as wind or water. For example, there are sculptures that have moving parts.

Theo Jansen (1948–) is a Dutch scientist and artist who builds huge sculptures. People call his art "strandbeests." This is because his sculptures move like animals in the wind.

SPEEDING CAR STUNT RAMP

Roll cars down a ramp to copy Galileo, one of the greatest scientists of all time!

A 17th century painting showing Galileo demonstrating his discovery.

GALILEO GALILEI

(1564–1642)

Galileo Galilei was a great Italian scientist. He was always asking questions, experimenting, and testing.

One of his many interests was rolling balls and other objects down slopes. He figured out how objects **accelerate** as they roll downhill or fall. They didn't just speed up a little bit. They kept getting faster and faster!

WHAT YOU NEED

- cardboard box
- marker
- craft knife or scissors
- large sheets of strong, flexible card stock
- packing tape or duct tape
- long piece of card stock from a large cardboard box
- a toy car

1&2

Step 1

Draw a curved line on the side of the cardboard box. With an adult's help, cut along the curve. Cut off the rest of the side of the box.

Step 2

Use the piece you have cut off as a template to draw the same curve on the other side of the box. Cut along the curve. Cut off the ends of the box so you have a curved shape at the top of the box.

3

Step 3

Take a large piece of card stock. Cut a piece to fit along the curve. Gently bend the card stock and tape it to the box.

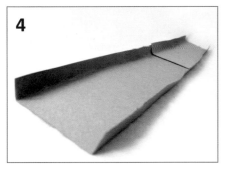

6

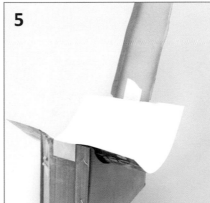

5

4

Step 4

To make a speed ramp, use a piece of stiff card stock. This should be 3 to 6 feet (1 to 2 m) long and 3 to 4 inches (8 to 10 cm) wide. (The length of the ramp can be two pieces joined together.) Fold the edges up to make walls along the ramp almost 0.5 inches (1.25 cm) high.

Step 5

Rest one end of the long ramp on a windowsill, table, or chair. Use tape to hold it in place. Line the other end up with the curved ramp. Tape them together to make a smooth join.

Step 6

Try rolling toy cars down the ramp, first from lower on the ramp, then from higher up. How fast do they go? How high do they have to start on the ramp to fly off?

PICKING UP SPEED

As Galileo found, the farther an object rolls down, the faster it goes. The cars roll downward because gravity pulls them to the ground. When the cars are moving, gravity adds to their speed.

When cars roll from higher on the ramp, they should pick up enough speed to fly off.

BEAT DE CREED!

Stunt drivers make car jumps like this in real life. Top stunt driver Jacquie de Creed beat the distance record in 1983 with an amazing 232-foot (71-m) jump. That's like jumping 18 cars lined up end-to-end. If you have enough toy cars, line them up between the ramps and see if you can beat that!

Try making a landing ramp, too. See if you can make a car safely jump the gap and land.

NEWTON'S CRADLE

Newton's cradle is a famous science toy. It is easy to make and interesting to watch.

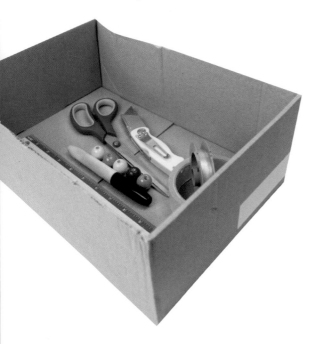

WHAT YOU NEED

- a small, strong cardboard box without a lid
- strong scissors or craft knife
- ruler
- marker pen
- at least 6.5 feet (2 m) of beading thread or fine string
- five large, heavy, round beads made of plastic, wood, or metal (not glass), with large holes
- tape

CHRISTIAAN HUYGENS

(1629–1695)

Christiaan Huygens was a Dutch scientist, known for his work on space. He also explored the science of forces and movement. Sir Isaac Newton, a famous scientist, had an impact on his work.

Huygens built a device to show how **motion** passes from one object to another. This device had swinging balls that crashed into each other. The invention is still a popular toy today.

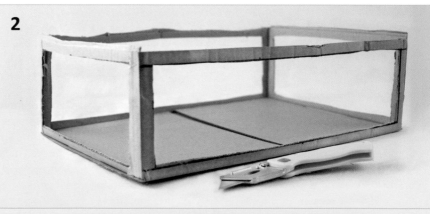

Step 1
Use the ruler and marker to draw a frame on each side of the box, about 0.5 inches (1 cm) in from the edge all around.

Step 2
With an adult to help, carefully cut along the lines with a craft knife or scissors. Remove a large rectangle from each side of the box. You will have a simple frame at the end.

Step 3

Cut five pieces of thread. They should each be about 16 inches (40 cm) long. Take one piece and thread it through a bead. Then thread it around and through again, so the bead stays in the middle of the thread. Repeat this for the rest of the beads and thread.

Step 4

Now tie the threads to the sides of the frame. The beads should hang down in the middle. Use knots that you can loosen or tighten easily. When all five beads are in place, loosen or tighten the threads so the beads are all touching in a row.

Step 5

Tie the knots tightly or use tape to hold them in place. Trim off any extra thread. Test the cradle by pulling a bead at one end away from the others and letting it drop back toward them.

PASSING IT ON

If your invention works, your first bead will stop when it hits the next one. When this happens, the bead at the other end will move away instead. The three beads in the middle will stay in place. This is because the **energy** passes through all the beads until the end. At the end, there is room for the bead to move. We call this the **conservation of momentum**. This means that movement energy does not disappear, but can pass from one object to another. The conservation of momentum was first discovered by Sir Isaac Newton.

MAKING FLIGHT

The Montgolfier brothers used paper to make their first hot air balloons. You can do the same.

An engraving showing the first human flight, on November 21, 1783.

JOSEPH-MICHEL MONTGOLFIER

(1740–1810)

JACQUES-ÉTIENNE MONTGOLFIER

(1745–1799)

Joseph and Étienne Montgolfier were brothers. Their family ran a paper-making business. The brothers worked on hot air balloons after Joseph saw how smoke from a fire made cloth rise upward. Using paper and cloth, the brothers experimented with bigger boxes and bags. They used smoke from fire to make the boxes rise. This was how they made the hot air balloon.

By September 1783, the hot air balloons were big enough to fit animals. In November 1783, people flew in a hot air balloon for the first time.

WHAT YOU NEED

- four large sheets of tissue paper
- marker
- scissors
- glue stick or PVA glue
- thin card stock
- hairdryer

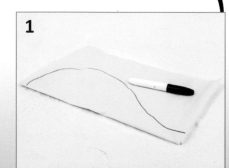

1

Step 1

Open up your tissue paper. Put the sheets in a pile on top of each other. Fold the whole pile in half. Use the marker to draw half of a long, narrow balloon shape.

2

Step 2

Holding all the paper together at the folded side, cut along the line. This will make four balloon shapes. Separate the shapes and fold them in half again.

3

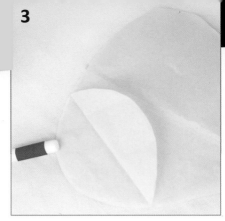

Step 3

On the first piece of paper, put a thin layer of glue around the edge of one half. Place another folded piece on top, so that the two edges stick together.

4

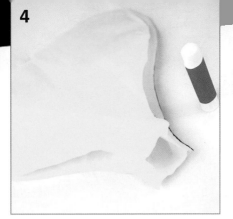

Step 4

Repeat with the next three pieces. Finally, fold the two remaining cut edges back. Glue them together as well. Glue adds weight, so try not to use too much.

5

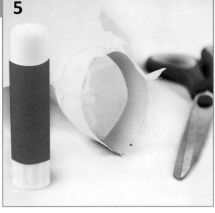

Step 5

Glue shut any gaps at the top of your balloon. Cut a strip of card stock about 1 inch (2.5 cm) wide. Glue it in a ring shape around the opening at the bottom of the balloon.

6

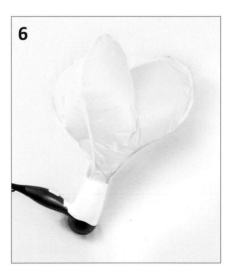

Step 6

Once the glue is dry, hold the balloon up and keep it flat. Ask an adult to turn the hairdryer on a low setting. Use the hot air to fill the balloon. This will happen quite fast. Once it's full of hot air, let it go!

> If it doesn't work very well, this could be because you're already in a warm room. It might work better somewhere cooler.

WHY DOES IT FLY?

Even though the Montgolfier brothers' balloons worked well, they didn't understand why. They thought that smoky fires made a type of gas that made the balloon rise.

It isn't smoke that makes hot air balloons fly. It is actually heat. Hot air is more spread out and lighter than cooler air. Since the hot air is lighter than the air around it, the cooler air sinks down. This pushes hot air up, taking the balloon with it.

PRESSURE DIVER

Make a diving octopus that sinks and floats with the squeeze of a bottle.

> My invention isn't about cold or heat, but about the resistance to **compression**.
> – *Raffaello Magiotti*

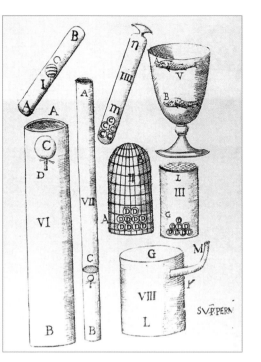

A picture from Magiotti's book, Water's Resistance to Compression, *showing different designs for the Cartesian diver.*

RAFFAELLO MAGIOTTI

(1597–1656)

Magiotti created a device now called the Cartesian diver. (In the past, it was called the Cartesian devil.) Magiotti made it to show that water is harder to push together than air. His creation is still used as a toy and science experiment today.

WHAT YOU NEED

- rubber glove
- scissors
- plastic medicine dropper
- sticky tack
- permanent marker
- waterproof tape or duct tape
- large clear plastic bottle with lid
- large bowl
- water

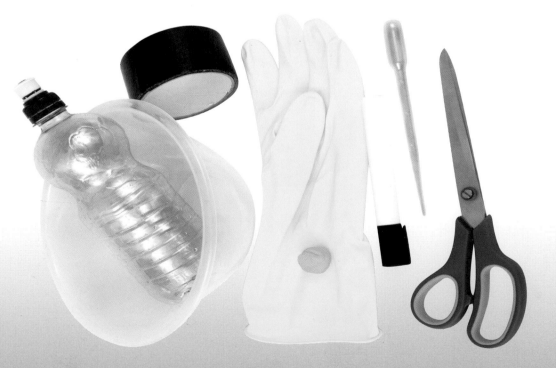

1

Step 1
With an adult to help, cut most of the long tube off the plastic dropper. Then cut off the smallest finger off the rubber glove.

2

Step 2
Cut off the tip of the finger to leave a small hole. Cut the lower end of the glove finger into octopus legs. Press a ring of sticky tack around the lower end of the dropper to make it heavier.

3

Step 3
Stretch the cut glove over the dropper and tape it in place with a small piece of strong tape. Add eyes using the marker.

4

Step 4
Fill your bottle with water right to the brim. Fill the bowl with water, too. You now need to put some water inside your octopus, so that it floats a little.

Step 5
Use the dropper to suck up some water. Leave some air inside. Put the dropper in the bowl. If it sinks, squeeze a little water out. The dropper needs to float, so that most of it hangs below the water's surface.

5

6

Step 6
When your octopus is ready, push it into the bottle of water. Fill the water to the brim and put the lid on tight. Squeeze the bottle with both hands to make the octopus dive. Let go to make it float again.

UP AND DOWN

What's going on? The octopus floats at first because of its **density**. The density is how much something weighs for its size. If an object is small and heavy it has a higher density. The density of the octopus is less than the density of the water.

When you squeeze the bottle, you squeeze the water inside, too. It is very hard to push water together when it is in a smaller space. Since the bottle is full, the only place for the water to go is into the diver.

The diver has an air bubble inside. Air is less dense than water. The water squeezes the air and it becomes smaller. Now the diver has more water in it, so its density is greater. This makes the octopus sink. When you let go, the squeezed air pushes some of the water back out, helping it float up again.

13

ROCKET POWER

Fire rockets by using the "springiness" of air!

"There is a Spring, or Elastical power in the Air we live in."
— *Robert Boyle*

SQUEEZING THE AIR

These pictures show how Boyle's tube worked. He sealed the tube at the curved end. The tube contained some mercury, trapping a little air. Boyle added more mercury to see what would happen.

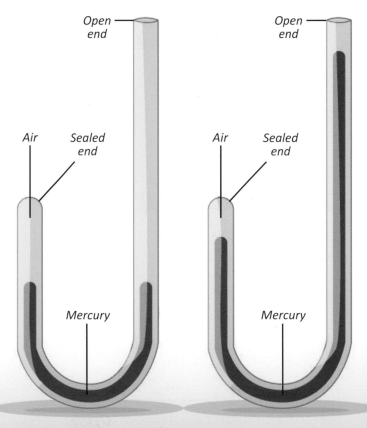

Open end

Air

Sealed end

Mercury

When Boyle added more mercury, it pushed on the air pocket. This squashed the air and made it smaller. The air "bounced" and pushed back, like a spring.

ROBERT BOYLE

(1627–1691)

Irish-born Robert Boyle was a scientist. He explored many things, including chemicals, forces, sound, light, freezing, and **air pressure**. He was especially interested in how to **compress** and squeeze air. He made a J-shaped tube with a pocket of air in the end. He used mercury (a heavy liquid metal) to push on the air. Boyle found that the more you squeeze air and put it under pressure, the more it pushes back. The movement is just like a bouncy spring.

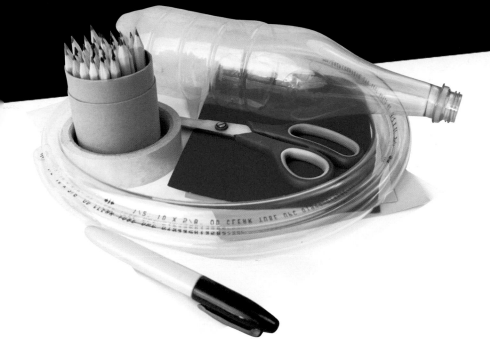

WHAT YOU NEED

- paper and card stock
- a piece of plastic tubing, around 3 feet (1 m) long and almost 1 inch (2 cm) wide
- marker
- scissors
- coloring pens or pencils
- a large plastic soda bottle
- strong tape or duct tape
- a computer and printer (optional)

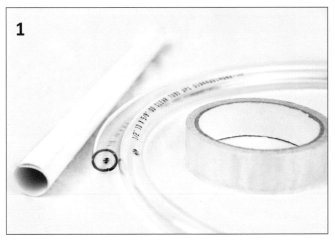

1

Step 1

Take a piece of paper. Roll it around the end of the plastic tubing to make a rocket body that's just slightly wider than the plastic tubing. Attach the paper rocket with tape.

2

Step 2

Find a round object, such as a roll of tape. Using more paper, draw around it to make a half-circle shape.

Step 3

Cut out the half circle. Curl it into a cone for the end of the rocket. Use tape to hold it together. Attach it to the top of your rocket.

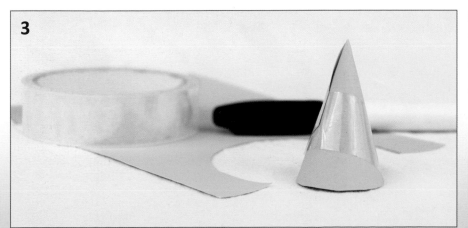

3

Soda bottles work best, as they are stronger than other bottles.

Step 4

Cut three or four triangles or curved fin shapes from card stock. Use tape to stick them onto the sides of the rocket near the bottom. Draw on windows and decorations, if you like.

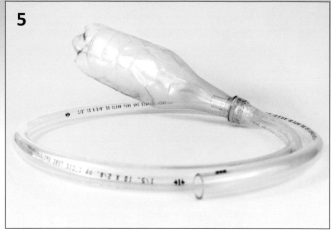

Step 5

If there is a lid, take it off the bottle. Insert the plastic tubing into the top of the bottle, if possible. If the tubing does not fit inside the bottle, join the bottle opening and the tube together with tape.

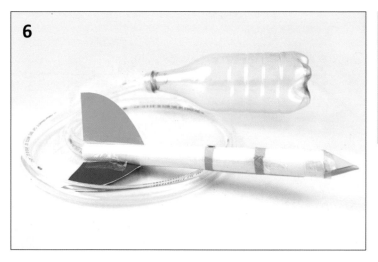

BE CAREFUL!

If it works, the rocket will move fast. Don't aim the rocket at other people, animals, or anything breakable! If possible, test it in a big room or outdoors to see how far it will go.

Step 6

With the help of an adult, test your rocket. Put the bottle on the floor and fit the rocket onto the other end of the tube. Aim the rocket and fire it by stomping hard on the bottle.

Step 7

To reuse the shooter, blow into the tube and reinflate the bottle.

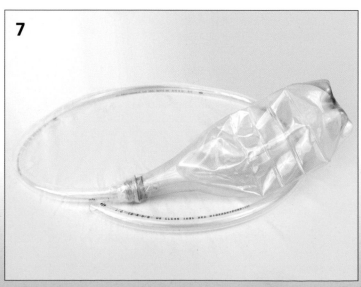

Step 8

Draw targets onto circles of paper or print photos from the Internet that you can use. You can print planets, moons, or other spacecraft. Give each photo a score number. With the help of an adult, stick them to a wall or large cardboard box. Take turns aiming at your targets. Keep score. You can even have each player make and decorate their own rocket!

INFLATABLE SCIENCE

You can feel the effect of air's "spring" when you blow up a balloon or bouncy castle. As you force more and more air into the space, you are putting it under pressure. When you press down or bounce on it, you can feel the air inside pushing back.

AIR PRESSURE POWER

When you stomp on the bottle, you squish the air inside and put it under pressure. This makes the **molecules** move closer to each other and the air pushes hard against the container it is in. Since the air can't escape from the bottle, it zooms down the tube. This forces the rocket to launch at a high speed.

Imagine if the bottle had water in it. This is much harder to squish. You wouldn't be able to stomp it flat as quickly as your current invention. The air would move slowly and the water would come out of the tube slowly, too. It's the sudden squeezing of the air that puts the air under pressure and makes it push outward again.

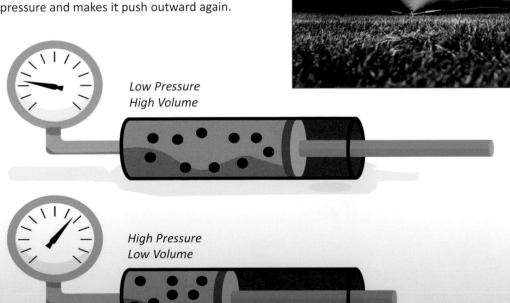

When the air is under less pressure, the molecules are more spread out, and don't push as hard.

*Low Pressure
High Volume*

When the air is squeezed, the molecules are forced together and push back harder.

*High Pressure
Low Volume*

FLOATING ON AIR

Make an easy model hovercraft that works like the real thing!

"People think there aren't more inventions to invent, but there are."
– Christopher Cockerell

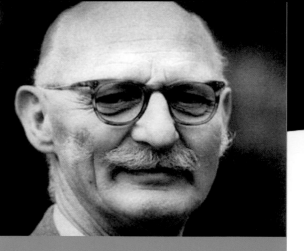

SIR CHRISTOPHER COCKERELL

(1910–1999)

In the early 1950s, British engineer and boat-builder Christopher Cockerell invented the hovercraft. The hovercraft is a type of boat that moves fast. This is because air moves underneath the boat to lessen resistance between the boat and the water.

People already talked about blowing air under a boat to do this, but there were difficulties. It was hard to get air under and stop it from escaping too fast. Cockerell built a model using a coffee tin, a cat food tin, and an air blower. He didn't only fill a space under the object in his tests. He also had moving air flow through a narrow gap around the sides. This made it push down harder. From this idea, Cockerell developed a full-sized hovercraft.

Cockerell's hovercraft SR-N1 on the Thames River in London, UK, 1959

WHAT YOU NEED

- an old, unwanted CD
  (if you don't have any, try a thrift shop)
- paper
- scissors
- colored markers or pencil crayons
- glue stick
- spout-shaped lid from a water bottle
- strong glue or a hot glue gun
- a balloon

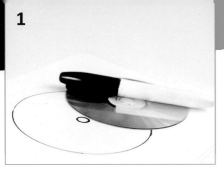

1

Step 1

Draw around the CD onto a piece of paper, including the hole in the middle. Cut out the circle and the hole. Draw a design on the paper.

2

Step 2

Use the glue stick to attach your design onto the CD, making sure it is well glued all around the middle. Leave it to dry completely.

3

Step 3

With an adult to help, use strong glue or a hot glue gun to glue the spout over the central hole in the CD. Make sure it is well glued all around. Leave it to dry.

4

Step 4

Blow up the balloon and twist the opening around a few times to hold the air in. Stretch the opening over the bottle spout. Put the hovercraft on a smooth floor or table.

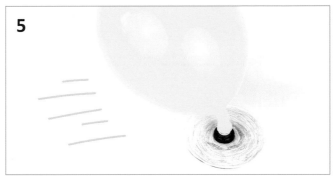

5

Step 5

To start the hovercraft, untwist the balloon so the air can flow out. Give the hovercraft a gentle push, and see how far it goes!

MIND THE GAP!

Try to push your CD along without the balloon. It will soon stop because of friction with the ground. Friction is a dragging, gripping force that is created when materials rub together. Think of how much slower your hands move when you rub them together. That's friction!

It's the same with a boat on water. Friction between the hull and the water creates **drag**. This slows the boat down. A hovercraft reduces drag by blowing a layer of air between the surfaces. Air contains fewer molecules than solids or liquids because it is a gas. Fewer molecules mean less friction.

Cockerell's hovercraft directed air along narrow paths to make it blow harder. This lifted the hovercraft higher. In the CD version, the air blows through the narrow hole in the middle, pushing the CD off the ground in a similar way.

*Hovercrafts are **amphibious**. This means they can travel over both land and water.*

WHALE RACE

Use the discoveries of Agnes Pockels to race whales over a tray of water.

"I have discovered the abnormal behaviour of the water surface.
— Agnes Pockels"

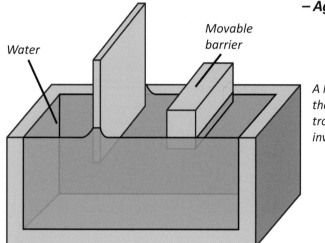

Water

Movable barrier

*A later version of the **surface tension** trough Pockels invented and built*

WHAT YOU NEED

- a large, shallow tray, such as a baking tray
- dishwashing liquid
- a pitcher of water
- colored markers or pencil crayons
- cotton swabs
- thin card stock
- scissors
- a saucer

AGNES POCKELS

(1862–1935)

German experimenter Agnes Pockels wanted to study science. At the time, most universities weren't open to women.

Her brother went to university. Agnes borrowed his books. She did her own experiments. She explored water and surface tension. Surface tension is a force that makes water molecules pull towards each other. The tension creates a "skin" on the surface of the water. It can hold up small objects.

For her experiments, Agnes invented a device to measure surface tension. She called it the Pockels trough.

1

Step 1
Put the tray on a solid, flat surface. Carefully fill it with water using the pitcher. Wait for the water to settle down and become still.

2

Step 2
On a piece of card stock, draw or trace a whale shape like this. Put a notch in the middle of its tail. Cut it out, keeping it as flat as possible.

3

Step 3
Make a whale for each person who wants to race. You can color them in, add eyes, and number them so you can tell whose is whose.

4

Step 4
Put some dishwashing liquid on the saucer. Have the cotton swabs ready. If you don't have any cotton swabs, you can use the blunt ends of pencils.

5

Step 5
Put the whales in the water at one end of the tray. To start the race, each person dips their cotton swab in the dishwashing liquid. Then they attach it to the notch on the back of their whale. Now watch your whales race!

SURFACE MOTION

Surface tension is all about force. Water molecules have a force that pulls them to each other. Inside the water, the molecules pull in all directions. Outside the water, they pull in and sideways. This creates a barrier. This is also why a surface can hold up small objects, like pins.

Adding a **detergent** to the water reduces surface tension behind the whale. The water molecules move toward the detergent and farther away from each other. At the same time, the surface tension in front of the whale is still strong. The water surface there pulls away from the detergent and takes the whale with it.

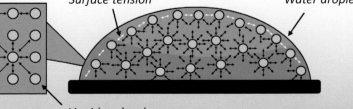

Surface tension

Water droplet

Liquid molecules

TIP!
If the whales start to get soggy, leave them to dry out, or just make some more.

PENDULUM ART

Create amazing art using a pendulum.

MAX ERNST

(1891–1976)

German painter, sculptor, and writer Max Ernst loved creating new ways to make art. One of the many things he tried was swinging a paint can with a hole in it back and forth to create loops of paint. Ernst called the looping movement "oscillation."

The invention itself was a type of **pendulum**. After using the invention, Ernst would then add colors and other things to the picture.

WHAT YOU NEED

- a door frame
- lots of newspaper
- tape
- an empty squeeze bottle with a lid, such as a dishwashing liquid bottle
- strong scissors
- hole punch
- string
- thumbtack
- water-based paint (either premixed or powder paint) in different colors
- plastic container
- spoon
- large pieces of plain paper

Step 1
First, spread a thick layer of newspaper on the floor, under and up the sides of the door frame. Keep it in place with tape.

Step 2
Make sure your squeeze bottle and lid are clean. With an adult to help, cut off the base of the bottle. Use a hole punch to make two holes in the bottle, near where the base has been cut off.

2

Step 3
Cut a piece of string about 8 feet (2.5 m) long. Thread it through the holes in the bottle. Tie the end so the bottle can hang up.

3

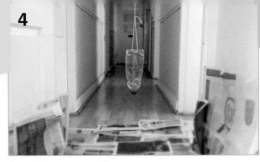

Step 4

Ask an adult to attach the other end of the string to the door frame with a thumbtack. The bottle should hang upside down about 4 to 8 inches (10–20 cm) off the ground.

Step 5

Put plenty of paint in the plastic container. Add water bit by bit, mixing until you have a thick but runny liquid paint.

Step 6

Make sure the lid is shut. Pour the paint into the squeeze bottle. With clean, dry hands, spread out a large piece of paper under the bottle.

Step 7

Pull the bottle slightly to one side. Open the lid, then let the bottle swing over the paper. Give it a slight push to the side so it moves in a circle or oval, dripping paint as it goes.

Step 8

When you're happy with the painting, stop the bottle and close the lid. If you like, you can try adding more colors. It will take several hours to dry.

SWINGING SCIENCE

A pendulum swings because of the force of gravity. Gravity pulls it down, while momentum keeps it moving. The way Earth spins also affects it. As time passes, resistance slows the pendulum down. This also changes the pattern.

This giant pendulum is found in a museum in Valencia, Spain. The rotation of Earth makes the pendulum move in different directions. The pendulum knocks the balls down.

KINETIC CREATIONS

Build a sculpture that moves and spins in the slightest breeze.

WHAT YOU NEED

- a tall glass bottle
- a cork that fits in the bottle
- straight pins
- small beads
- drinking straws
- Styrofoam craft balls in different sizes
- glue
- scissors
- lightweight materials, such as card stock, aluminum foil, corks, and feathers

LIN EMERY

(1928–)

American artist Lin Emery is a leading sculptor. She makes 3-D **kinetic** works of art powered by water. Some of her art moves in the wind, twirling and spinning around, but it always stays in balance.

1&2

3

Step 1

Stand your bottle on a flat, firm surface. Push the cork into the top, so that it's sticking out. This is the base for your sculpture.

Step 2

With the help of an adult, push a pin right through the middle of one of the straws. Thread two or three beads onto the pin below the straw. Push the pin into the middle of the cork. Make sure that the straw can spin around freely.

Step 3

Ask an adult to help you use the scissors to make a small hole in a Styrofoam ball. Put a drop of glue in the hole. Push it onto one end of the straw you have already added to the bottle. Do the same on the other end, too.

4

5

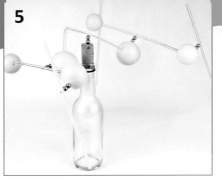

6

Step 4

With the help of an adult, push a pin through a new straw. Thread some beads onto the pin and push the pin into the Styrofoam ball. The new straw should also spin around. On the other end, add a new straw to the Styrofoam ball.

Step 5

Keep adding more straws in the same way so you have several branches. Try experimenting with different lengths of straws. You can put the pins in different positions. Spin them as you add them to check that the parts do not crash into each other.

Step 6

Add interesting shapes or objects to the moving ends of the straws. You can use pieces cut out of cardboard or foil. Try different sizes and weights to make the sculpture balance.

Lin Emery's stainless steel sculpture, Deva (1986), at Marina Bay in Singapore

Here are some ideas for shapes and patterns.

> "The elements are derived from nature, and I borrow natural elements—wind, water, magnets—to set them in motion.
> — *Lin Emery*

IN THE BALANCE

A sculpture like this will stay balanced as long as the weight is equal on each side of the central pin. Each moving arm of the sculpture needs to balance the same way.

Emery builds her sculptures so that even when all the parts are moving, the balance stays equal. This can take some time to get right! When it works, the sculpture will move in a breeze or when you blow it.

A Rube Goldberg machine uses many forces to complete one job!

"The machines are a symbol of man's capacity for exerting maximum effort to achieve minimal results."
– Rube Goldberg

RUBE GOLDBERG

(1883–1970)

Rube Goldberg was an American cartoonist, engineer, and sculptor. He created funny and complicated machines. They used many movements to do a task. For example, pouring a cup of tea or ringing a bell.

Today, Rube Goldberg machines are popular. They are in advertisements, games, and videos. There are even competitions to see who can build the best one!

This Rube Goldberg machine has lots of parts for the simple task of turning on a light.

WHAT YOU NEED

You can make a Rube Goldberg machine with all kinds of everyday objects. This list has some of the most common and useful items people have. You can add others, as long as they're not breakable or dangerous. Avoid anything sharp, hot, breakable, or messy. Also check with an adult before taking things to use. Here are the items we used for our Rube Goldberg machine:

- balloon
- empty paper towel tube
- paper cups
- a toy car
- needles or pins
- sticky tack
- skewer
- bead with groove for pulley
- string
- two water bottles
- cardboard box
- dominoes
- small drum stick or similar object
- several small books
- card stock
- tape
- a large marble

To design and build the machine, you'll also need tools and supplies, such as:

- pencil and paper
- strong packing tape
- scissors
- glue

Step 1

Like Rube Goldberg himself, you need to plan out your ideas on paper. This makes it much easier to build your machine. Start by choosing the task you want to complete, such as ringing a bell or popping a balloon.

Step 2

Now work backward from your task. Plan your actions. Each action must happen based on the action before it. For example:

TASK: POP A BALLOON

To pop the balloon, a toy car with a needle taped to the front rolls down a slope and hits the balloon.

To push the car down the slope, a weight falls into a cup. This pulls up a lever under the car.

To push the weight into the cup, a row of dominoes gets knocked over.

To knock the dominoes over, the first one gets hit by a stick.

To push the stick over, a line of books falls onto each other.

To make the books fall, a ball rolls down a slope.

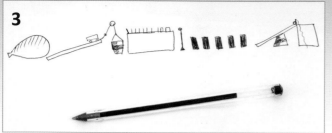

Step 3

It may also help to draw a sketch of your machine, with arrows and labels to show how it will all work. You can then use this to help while building.

Step 4

A good way to make a slope is to cut open an empty paper towel roll. Using a paper cup, put the roll on an angle. You will need to cut a slot out of the paper cup to make your slope stay.

Step 5

Attach a ball of sticky tack onto the car. With an adult to help, stick a needle into it with the pointed end outward. This makes a balloon-popper.

Step 6

Make a pulley with a bead on a skewer. This will need to hang between two bottles of water. Loop some string over the bead. Tie one end to the cup and the other end to a paper tab, which fits under the car.

Step 7

Line a row of dominoes on top of the box. Arrange them so that when they fall, the last one will fall into the cup.

Step 8

Stand a drum stick on the ground where it will knock over the first domino. Secure it with sticky tack.

Step 9

Line up a row of small books behind the drum stick.

Step 10

Set up another slope with a large marble at the top of it, ready to roll down. Use a piece of paper to block it.

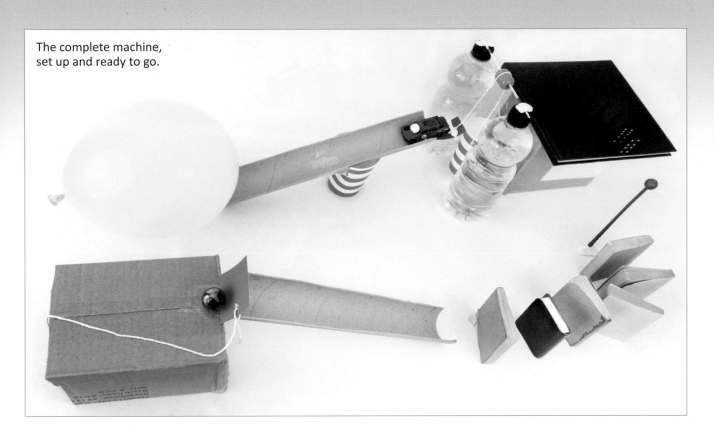

The complete machine, set up and ready to go.

FORCES AT WORK

A Rube Goldberg machine moves force from one end to the other. A good one uses as many different forces as possible. It can include gravity, swings, magnets, friction, balance, and air pressure. The other projects in this book can give you more ideas.

This example of a Rube Goldberg machine uses weights, a pulley system, and a spring to blow up a balloon.

GLOSSARY

accelerate To increase in speed

air pressure The pushing force created by the weight of the air in the atmosphere

air resistance A force that slows down an object as it moves through air

amphibious Able to travel through both air and water

applied force A force that has a direct impact on an object. This is force that is usually applied by a person or another object.

compress To squeeze, press, or make smaller

compression The application of external force onto something, causing its particles to squeeze closer together

conservation of momentum A law of physics that says momentum passes from one object into another

density The amount of matter a substance or object has compared to its volume

detergent A type of cleaning substance. For example, dishwashing detergent gets rid of grease and dirt from surfaces.

drag A force that slows down an object as it moves through a liquid or gas. Air resistance is a type of drag.

electric force A force between objects that has an electric charge. This is a pushing or pulling force.

energy The ability to do work or make things happen

force A push or pull that makes things move, stop, change direction, or change shape.

friction A force that grips things or slows things down. This happens when surfaces press or rub against each other.

gravity A force that pulls objects toward each other. The larger the object, the greater its force of gravity.

kinetic A kind of energy that comes from movement

molecules Tiny units made up of connected atoms. These make up substances.

momentum The tendency of a moving object to keep moving in the same direction

motion Another word for movement

pendulum A weight hanging from a fixed point and able to swing free

surface tension A pulling force between the molecules in a liquid. This makes the liquid behave as though it has a "skin" on its surface.

upthrust An upward force a liquid or gas creates on an object that is floating in it

FURTHER INFORMATION

WEBSITES ABOUT FORCES

Physics4Kids
www.physics4kids.com/index.html

NASA Space place: What is gravity?
http://spaceplace.nasa.gov/what-is-gravity/en

Explain That Stuff! Forces and Motion
www.explainthatstuff.com/motion.html

Science Trek: Forces and Motion Facts
http://idahoptv.org/sciencetrek/topics/
force_and_motion/facts.cfm

WEBSITES ABOUT MAKING

Tate Kids: Make
www.tate.org.uk/kids/make

PBS Design Squad Global
http://pbskids.org/designsquad

Instructables
www.instructables.com

Teachers Try Science: Kids Experiments
www.teacherstryscience.org/kids-experiments

WHERE TO BUY MATERIALS

Home Science Tools
www.homesciencetools.com

Staples
www.staples.com

The Home Depot
Tubing, wood, glue and, other hardware supplies
www.homedepot.com

BOOKS

Claybourne, Anna. *Gut-Wrenching Gravity and Other Fatal Forces*. Crabtree, 2013.

Sjonger, Rebecca. *Changing Matter in My Makerspace*. Crabtree, 2018.

Spilsbury, Richard. *Investigating Forces and Motion*. Crabtree, 2018.

PLACES TO VISIT

The Tech Museum of Innovation
www.thetech.org

Exploratorium
www.exploratorium.edu

Smithsonian National Air and Space Museum
http://airandspace.si.edu

INDEX